Document Exercise Workbook

For

WESTERN CIVILIZATION:

VOLUME 1: To 1715

Donna L. Van Raaphorst
Cuyahoga Community College

West/Wadsworth
I(T)P® An International Thomson Publishing Company

Belmont, CA • Albany, NY • Boston • Cincinnati • Johannesburg • London • Madrid • Melbourne
Mexico City • New York • Pacific Grove, CA • Scottsdale, AZ • Singapore • Tokyo • Toronto

Cover Image: *A thirteenth-century miniature depicting the siege and capture of Constantinople by the fourth crusade in 1204*, by permission of Bibliotheque Nationale, Paris.

Printed in Canada.
4 5 6 7 8 9 10

For more information, contact Wadsworth Publishing Company, 10 Davis Drive, Belmont, CA 94002, or electronically at http://www.wadsworth.com.

International Thomson Publishing Europe
Berkshire House
168-173 High Holborn
London, WC1V 7AA, United Kingdom

International Thomson Editores
Seneca, 53
Colonia Polanco
11560 México D.F. México

Nelson ITP, Australia
102 Dodds Street
South Melbourne
Victoria 3205 Australia

International Thomson Publishing Asia
60 Albert Street #15-01
Albert Complex
Singapore 189969

Nelson Canada
1120 Birchmount Road
Scarborough, Ontario
Canada M1K 5G4

International Thomson Publishing Southern Africa
Building 18, Constantia Square
138 Sixteenth Road, P.O. Box 2459
Halfway House, 1685 South Africa

International Thomson Publishing Japan
Hirakawa-cho Kyowa Building, 3F
2-2-1 Hirakawa-cho
Chiyoda-ku
Tokyo 102, Japan

Senior Developmental Editor: Sharon Adams Poore
Editorial Assistant: Melissa Gleason
Ancillary Coordinator: Rita Jaramillo
Print Buyer: Judy Inouye

ISBN 0-534-56083-0

For Paul, whose help along the way
would have made it eminently better.

Contents

Vol. I

Foreword

The genesis of this work has been twenty some years of classroom instruction. Throughout this time period my students have been my best teachers and in no case is this more so than with the revisions in this edition.

Many individuals helped to make these volumes possible. Of particular note are Clark Baxter and Linda Poirier.

Equally supportive were numerous individuals on the Western Campus Cuyahoga Community College. Of special note are my Provost, Mr. Ronald M. Sobel, my word processor, Ms. Elizabeth Russin, Ms. Mikki Shackelton, a former student and Mr. John Twist, book center manager. Last but not least I am particularly grateful to my trusted and true friend Mary Kay Howard of John Carroll University for our numerous "brainstorming sessions." Without their assistance, aid, and cooperation this work would not have been possible.

To The Student

This supplement was written with you in mind. Specifically, it was designed to complement the textbook you are reading in your Western Civilization course. This small volume includes some documents that you will find in your text and several that are not.

The method of organization is chronological and the exercises that accompany the documents will progress from the relatively simple to the far more complex. The documents reflect the wide range of materials historians use in attempting to reconstruct the past. If you begin using this supplement when your coursework commences and continue to use it throughout the duration of your survey study of Western Civilization, you will develop a better understanding of historical source materials and of how historians study history.

To The Instructor

The materials within are arranged in a typical chronological fashion, but this book attempts to be more than simply another collection of documents. It endeavors to engage the student in a study of the past through a series of carefully constructed exercises using primary sources. These exercises are intended to develop thinking skills appropriate to the study of history. As such, they progress from those relatively simple in nature to those far more complex. More importantly, the exercises are ultimately aimed, as Russel H. Hvolbek has aptly written, for "the primary purpose of teaching history and the humanities (which) is to make students more aware of how their lives connect to the past human experience." This objective cannot be achieved by simply acquiring a body of knowledge. Students will come much closer to this goal if they learn how to seek out information and if they learn how to use this information. Hvolbek informs us that this is our ultimate responsibility in reevaluating how we teach our discipline with the provocative title of his essay--"History and Humanities: Teaching as Destructive of Certainty." (AHA Perspectives, January, 1991)

Chapter I
The Nature of History

Before you read this important introductory chapter, write your definition of history on a piece of paper and then put your response aside. When you have finished reading this chapter, examine anew your original thoughts. Compare the differences you find. Think about these differences.

This simple exercise is intended to challenge your presumptions about history. History is not what many of you think it to be. It is not the acquisition of a body of information--names, dates, places, events--simply to be memorized and then shortly forgotten. History is much more. History is far more difficult, far more thought-provoking, far more profound, far more exciting, and more important, far more meaningful to your lives. In fact, one could argue that it is the most important subject you will ever study. When examined and understood properly, history provides us with insights into the fundamental questions that have always concerned humanity beginning with who am I and why am I here? When you understand history you will have become an informed, literate, insightful, thinking human being.

Understood in this way, history would be classified as part of a larger group of disciplines identified as the humanities. An even more thoughtful way to think of history, along with the other humanities, is as the <u>Report of the Colloquium on the Humanities and the American People</u>, has done:

> We identify them, rather, with certain ways of thinking--of inquiring, evaluating, judging, finding, and articulating meaning . . . . They are taken together, the necessary resources of a reflective approach to life. The value of a reflective approach can be best appreciated by considering the alternative: a life unilluminated by imagination, uninformed by history, unguided by reasoning--in short, the "unexamined life" that Socrates described as not worth living . . . .(1)

In order that these statements reflect more than grandiloquent expressions of a historian about their chosen discipline, three important questions must be addressed. They are the following: What is history?; How does the historian proceed?; and, What is history for?

A logical place to turn in your attempt to answer the first question, "What is history?," would be a dictionary of word origins or a book of word histories. In so doing you are examining the etymology of the word--its history or its origins. Etymologically, then, history simply denotes "knowledge." This should be interesting for you to discover because the most simplistic understanding of history is often that it is the accumulation of information. To arrive at the more complex aspects of our word, a more specific modern meaning must be uncovered.

The modern story (frequently another common definition of history) begins with the Greek word histor, meaning "learned man." In turn, histor is a descendant of the Indo-European word wid, which is defined as to "know" or "see." This led to the English word wit and the Latin word videre, meaning "see." From histor the word historia evolved and, for you, its meaning is of utmost significance. The definition of historia is "knowledge obtained by inquiring, or a written account of one's inquiries."(2) History, then is a process of inquiring. Specifically the historian, as well as the student of history, inquires into the past and records his or her findings.

Use of the word inquire says something important because it implies a process of asking questions that leads to an interpretation of the evidence. A process is doing and that is the essence of what this small book is trying to teach you--how to do history rather than be a passive recipient of information.(3) In order to do history, you must learn how to ask good questions. Obviously the historian (in this case you) proceeds by asking questions about things that happened in the past. Simple enough, right? Not really, not after you have thought about it momentarily. Whether you realize it or not, some questions are not appropriate to the discipline of history. For example, you would not ask questions about the past failure of your compact disk player to work properly. Questions not germane to humans, their activities, their institutions, their culture, their economy are inappropriate for historical investigation. However, the main difficulty confronting historians isn't eliminating unimportant or unanswerable questions. It is, instead, choosing from among the important ones.

Generally speaking, the important questions historians ask of their evidence, called sources, are--the who; the why; the when; the where; and, most important of all, the so what? Reflect for a moment on this as you read the following ideas of the well-known Yale historian, Professor Robin W. Winks, on history and asking good questions:

> History is, fundamentally, applied common sense. History begins in the fascination of discreet fact. History is curiosity, a desire to poke and pry to get answers to questions. History is asking good questions. [But not all these questions will, or should, be answered--save one.] The most challenging question, a damaging question that should be asked of any lecturer who ever spelled out a theory, is to look them straight in the eye and say, "Yes, but so what?" It's a paralyzing question. It's soul-destroying. And yet the historian must be able to answer the question.(4)

Mention of sources has been made several times. Historical sources are found in a variety of forms and places. In fact, historical sources, evidence of the past, are everywhere around you. Here are some examples--letters, maps, photographs, cemeteries, reports, personal diaries, buildings, recordings. The list is all but endless, but most traditionally the historian works with written sources, which are commonly referred to as documents. A document is defined as "a thing existing here and now, of such a kind that the historian, by thinking about it, can get answers to the questions he asks about past events."(5)

Generally speaking, when the historian uses the word document, he or she means "primary source" material. This means a record of the actual words of someone who either participated or witnessed whatever is being described. Primary sources are one of two basic types of evidence the historian uses in reconstructing the past. The other is referred to as a "secondary source." A secondary source is the interpretation of an individual who did not participate or witness whatever is being descibed, but who investigated the primary source(s), e.g., an historian.

If good questions need to be formulated in order to interpret your source materials, you also need to examine your evidence carefully for bias, for accuracy, for content. Suppose you were to write a biography of Winston Churchill. Would it be wise to rely only on funeral orations; family memoirs; the opinions of political opponents? Why not? In other words, as you evaluate your sources, you need to consider the circumstances under which they were written. What might have been the motive of the author? What was the relationship of the writer to the individual in question? What was the relationship of the author to the person, the place, the event, the time in question? One source needs to be checked against another to try and establish as full and as accurate a picture of the past as possible. As possible, of course, implies incomplete. Did you ever realize or consider this fact?

Think of it in terms of the philosophical issue of the forest and the tree. In that forest how many trees exist? How many of those trees can you actually observe? Even if you say one and you are standing under it, how many of its limbs can you observe; how many of its actual branches; and, how many of its leaves? When you consider this, you can perhaps begin to comprehend the true meaning of as possible and incomplete. The author Janet Malcolm expressed it beautifully when she wrote, "in a work of nonfiction we almost never know the truth of what happened. The ideal of unmediated reporting is regularly achieved only in fiction, where the writer faithfully reports on what is going on in his imagination. . . ."(6)

One final aspect concerning the question of how the historian proceeds needs to be addressed. That question concerns itself with the matter of organization--how are the source materials discovered about the past to be organized in such a way that significant information becomes apparent? Examination of this issue has demonstrated certain basic human activities that clearly stand out and answer basic questions. These activities fall into the following categories: <u>political</u>; <u>economic</u>; <u>social</u>; <u>religious</u>; <u>scientific</u>; <u>cultural</u>; and, <u>intellectual</u>. Some might also include <u>technological</u> and <u>artistic</u>. Remember these as you progress through the various exercises in this book and as you study and learn for your history course.

Almost fifty years ago now, R. G. Collingwood, a Professor of Philosophy at Oxford and a practicing historian, asked and answered the final question under consideration in this chapter: "What is history for?" Conceding it to be the most difficult and highly individualistic in nature, Collingwood nonetheless wrote,

> My answer is that history is 'for' human self-knowledge. It is generally thought to be of importance to man that he should know himself: where knowing himself means knowing not his merely personal peculiarities . . . but his nature as man. Knowing yourself means knowing first, what it is to be a man; secondly, knowing what it is to be the kind of man you are; and thirdly, knowing what it is to be the man <u>you</u> are and nobody else is. Knowing yourself means knowing what you can do; and since nobody knows what he can do until he tries, the only clue to what man can do is what man has done. The value of history, then, is that it teaches us what man has done and thus what man is.(7)

Endnotes

1. Merrill D. Peterson, <u>The Humanities and the American Promise</u>, Report of the Colloquium on the Humanities and the American People (Austin, Texas: Texas Committee for the Humanities, 1987), 2-3.

2. <u>Dictionary of Word Origins</u>, s.v. "history," and <u>The Merriam-Webster New Book of Word Histories</u>, s.v. "history."

3. Finlay McQuade, "What is <u>doing</u> a discipline?" (Waltham, MA: The College Board, n.d.).

4. "For Sleuth, History is Where He Finds It," <u>The Plain Dealer</u>, 11 February 1990.

5. R. G. Collingwood, <u>The Idea of History</u> (New York: Oxford University Press, 1946; A Galaxy Book, 1956), 10.

6. Janet Malcolm, "The Silent Woman - III," <u>The New Yorker</u>, 23 & 30 August 1993, 138.

7. Collingwood, <u>The Idea of History</u>, 10.

Chapter II
Applying the Basics to Historical Sources

Now that you have addressed the essentials and come to terms with a new understanding and appreciation of the complexities of history, you should be ready to actually try your hand at doing some history. In this chapter your exercises will deal with two types of source materials. Scholars of very early history frequently have to rely on other than strictly written materials like documents. It is important for you to understand how to use a variety of source materials even in your attempt to understand the modern world. Consider how many letters you have written lately? Do you keep a written diary?

Your first exercise will focus on a coin, what is commonly classified as an artifact. Coins have a history of their own; one that begins in the western part of Asia Minor in an early civilization called Lydia. Establishing a brief hegemony over Asia Minor from the middle of the 7th to the middle of the 6th century B.C., the Lydians are believed to have invented metallic coinage. Prior to this, jewelry was probably the closest thing to money.(1) Lydians are also responsible for establishing the first permanent retail shops and together these two important contributions to civilization played a role as catalyst in bringing about a commercial revolution helping to transform 6th century B.C. Greek civilization.

Let us suppose you find the coin pictured on the next page in the ruins of a very ancient civilization about which you know absolutely nothing. You are able to decipher the language for it is very similar to your own. However, you don't understand how this came to be. Study the coin carefully and then do the following:

1.   List five to ten things you believe you can determine about this civilization.

2.   Take your list and categorize it according to those most commonly used by historians to organize their information. Remember what they are?--political; economic; social; religious; scientific; cultural; and, intellectual.

Are you surprised by how much can be determined with one piece of evidence? Did you ever think of coins as an historical source? Actually, they are often invaluable to the historian. For instance, almost no records exist to inform us about the Parthian dynasty in 247 B.C. The Parthians were originally a nomadic people from central Asia, who at some point in history entered Iran (ancient Persia). Apparently they were at their peak of power about the end of the second century B.C. Tucked between two far greater powers--Rome to the west and China to the east--they were able to control at least a part of the great Silk Route and act as middle-men between their mightier neighbors. Inscriptions on coins and potsherds (pieces of broken earthen pots) have helped to corroborate the only other source materials available: the findings of archaeologists and subjective accounts of classical Greek and Roman texts.(2) Are you convinced?

Try working with a more conventional piece of historical evidence, an actual document and in this case a very famous early code of laws--the Code of Hammurabi. Much more can be found out about Hammurabi by reading and reviewing your textbook. As for the Code, it was cut in a diorite shaft nearly eight feet high and was discovered some time early in the 20th century by French archaeologists at a place called Susa, in modern-day Iran. Unknown persons had transported it there from Babylon.(3)

From this point on, whenever you are working with a document, always perform the following procedures:

- o   Have a dictionary by your side. You cannot understand a document if you do not understand the vocabulary.

- o   As you read through the document, circle all unfamiliar words and look them up in your dictionary.

- o   As you read through the document, look for the important ideas that relate to the question or questions you are seeking to answer (the who?; the why?; the when?; the where?; and the so what?). Underline them.

- o   Write these ideas out in your own words. In this way you will better understand them.

Remember these procedures as you make your way through the sections of the Code provided on the next few pages. Write and work on them as they are designed with that in mind.

DOCUMENT

The Code of Hammurabi

Prologue

When the lofty Anu, king of the Anunaki, and Enlil, lord of heaven and earth, who

determines the destinies of the land, committed the rule of all mankind to Marduk,

the first-born son of Ea, and made him great among the Igigi; when they pronounced

the lofty name of Babylon, made it great among the quarters of the world and in its midst established for him an everlasting kingdom whose foundations were firm as heaven and earth--at that time Anu and Enlil named me Hammurabi, the exalted prince, the worshipper of the gods, to cause righteousness to prevail in the land, to destroy the wicked and the evil, to prevent the strong from plundering the weak, to go forth like the sun over the black-headed race, to enlighten the land and to further the welfare of the people . . . .

The ancient seed of royalty, the powerful king, the sun of Babylon, who caused light to go forth over the lands of Sumer and Akkad; the king who caused the four quarters of the world to render obedience; the favorite of Innanna am I. When Marduk sent me to rule the people and to bring help to the land, I established law and justice in the language of the land and promoted the welfare of the people.

The Laws

25. If a fire break out in a man's house and a man who goes to extinguish it cast his eye on the household property of the owner of the house, and take the household property of the owner of the house, that man shall be thrown into the fire.

26. If either an officer or a constable who is ordered to go on an errand of the king do not go . . . that officer or constable shall be put to death . . . .

42. If a man rent a field for cultivation and do not produce any grain in the field, because he has not performed the necessary work on the field they shall convict him, and he shall give to the owner of the field grain on the basis of the adjacent fields.

87. If he put out money at interest, for one shekel of silver he shall receive one-fifth of a shekel as interest.

128. If a man take a wife and do not draw up a contract with her, that woman is not a wife.

150. If a man make his wife a present of field, garden, house, and goods and deliver to her a sealed deed, after the death of her husband, her children may not make any claim to her. The mother after her death may give them to her child who she loves, but to a brother she may not give them.

168. If a man set his face to disinherit his son and say to the judges, "I will disinherit my son," the judges shall inquire into his past, and if the son have not committed a crime sufficiently grave to cut him off from sonship, the father may not cut off his son from sonship.

12

196. If a man destroy the eye of another man, they shall destroy his eye.

197. If he break a man's bone, they shall break his bone.

198. If he destroy the eye of a common man or break a bone of a common man, he shall pay one mina of silver.

199. If he destroy the eye of a man's slave or break a bone of a man's slave, he shall pay one-half his price.

200. If a man knock out a tooth of a man of his own rank, they shall knock out his tooth.

201. If he knock out a tooth of a common man, he shall pay one-third mina of silver.

218. If a physician make a deep incision upon a man with his bronze lancet and cause the man's death, or operate on the eye socket of a man with his bronze lancet and destroy the man's eye, they shall cut off his hand.

229. If a builder erect a house for a man and do not make its construction firm, and the house which he built collapse and cause the death of the owner of the house, that builder shall be put to death.(4)

QUESTIONS

Now that you have read the document and followed the preceding steps, answer the three questions below:

1. Apply the categories used by the historian to organize information--what in the document is political history; economic history; social history; and so forth. For purposes of simplification, place abbreviations after appropriate sentences or statements in the Prologue and after each law in question eg. (p) political, (soc) social, (sci) scientific. Write directly in your workbook.

2. Upon completion of your categorization, write a short paragraph describing what you believe life in Hammurabi's Mesopotamia was like. Use as many of the categories as you can to provide as complete a picture of this society as you can.

3. Examine your results. Think about what you have done. Do you have a better understanding of history and what the historian does after completing this exercise?

Endnotes

1. Margaret Oliphant, <u>The Atlas of the Ancient World: Charting the Great Civilizations of the Past</u> (New York: Simon & Shuster, 1992), 67-69.

2. <u>Ibid</u>., 76.

3. George H. Knoles and Rixford K. Snyder, ed., <u>Readings In Western Civilization</u>, 3rd ed. (Chicago: J. B. Lippincott Company, 1960), 3.

4. Louis Cohn-Haft, ed., <u>Source Readings in Ancient History, Vol. I: The Ancient Near East and Greece</u> (New York: Macmillan Publishing Company, 1965), 81-84; 86; 89; 91; 93; 96-98; 102.

Chapter III
A Basic Historical Skill - Selection

Theocracy, monarchy, tyranny, oligarchy, democracy--are you able to properly define these important terms? Do you know from what ancient civilization these terms are derived? If you answered the Greeks, you are correct! And of all of them, we most closely associate the Greeks with the last, democracy. In fact, it is often stated that the ancient Greek polis of Athens was the cradle of democracy; that many of the political ideals developed therein--equality among the citizenry, respect for the law, regard for justice, liberty--have been shaping forces in history up to the present.

Let us suppose you wish to examine the veracity of this claim regarding Athens and democracy. How would you go about doing it using the evidence provided in the following documents? Remember to use your dictionary; to underline the key ideas; and, to put those ideas in your own words. Before you examine the three documents, carefully read the definition of democracy provided for your assistance.

The word democracy entered English in the sixteenth century from the French democratie; the word is Greek in origin, having been derived from demokratia, the root meanings of which are demos (people) and kratos (rule). Democracy refers to a form of government in which, in contradistinction to monarchies and aristocracies, the people rule. It entails a state in which there is some form of political equality among the people . . . .(1)

In the course of examining the definition of democracy, the three documents, and the questions that follow them, you will engage in a most fundamental historical skill, the skill of selection. Consider what should take place. You will enter into a dialogue with the documents--"a process by which the mind selects ever more accurately the sources that have significant meaning and relation to each other and at the same time refines the questions it needs to ask the sources."(2)

Think of it in another way by reflecting on the following problem relating to the Macedonian, Alexander the Great. Sometime in June, 323 B.C., Alexander, the man who extended Greek ideas and language to the ancient Near East, died. In that last year of his life, literally thousands upon thousands of things happened to him. Why have historians chosen to record so few of them?(3)

DOCUMENT 1

In the next place . . . . the fact that everywhere greater consideration is shown to the base, to poor people and to common folk, than to persons of good quality--so far from being a matter of surprise, this, as can be shown, is the keystone of the preservation of the democracy. It is these poor people, this common folk, this worse element, whose prosperity, combined with the growth of their numbers, enhances the democracy . . . .

What, then, I venture to assert is, that the People of Athens has no difficulty in recognizing which of its citizens are of the better sort and which the opposite. And so recognizing those who are serviceable and advantageous to itself, even though they be base, the People loves them; but the good folk they are disposed . . . to hate. This virtue of theirs, the People holds, is not engrained in their nature for any good to itself, but rather for its injury . . . . For my part, I pardon the People its own democracy, as, indeed it is pardonable in any one to do good to himself. But the man who, not being himself one of the People, prefers to live in a state democratically governed rather than in an oligarchical state may be said to smooth his own path towards iniquity. He knows that a bad man has a better chance of slipping through the fingers of justice in a democratic . . . state . . . .(4)

DOCUMENT 2

Our constitution does not copy the laws of neighbouring states; we are rather a pattern to others than imitators ourselves. Its administration favours the many instead of the few . . . . If we look to the laws, they afford equal justice to all in their private differences; if to social standing, advancement in public life falls to reputation for capacity, class considerations not being allowed to interfere with merit; nor again does poverty bar the way; if a man is able to serve the state, he is not hindered by obscurity of his condition. The freedom which we enjoy in our government extends also to our ordinary life. There, far from exercising a jealous surveillance over each other, we do not feel called upon to be angry with our neighbour for doing what he likes, or even to indulge in those injurious looks which cannot fail to be offensive, although they inflict no positive penalty. But all this ease in our private relations does not make us lawless as citizens. Against this fear is our chief safeguard, teaching us to obey the magistrates and the laws, particularly such as regard the protection of the injured, whether they are actually on the statute book, or belong to that code which, although unwritten, yet cannot be broken without acknowledged disgrace.(5)

DOCUMENT 3

Our commonwealth preserves its former frame,

Our common people are no more the same:

They that in skins and hides were rudely dress'd

Nor dreamt of law nor sought to be redress'd

By rules of right, but in the days of old

Flock'd to the town, like cattle to the fold,

Are now the brave and wise; and we, the rest,

(Their betters nominally, once the best)

Degenerate, debased, timid, mean!

Who can endure to witness such a scene?

Their easy courtesies, the ready smile,

Prompt to deride, to flatter, and beguile!

Their utter disregard of right or wrong,

Or truth or honour!--Out of such a throng

 (For any difficulties, any need,

For any bold design or manly deed)

Never imagine you can choose a just

Or steady friend, or faithful in his trust.

        But change your habits! Let them go their way!

Be condescending, affable, and gay! . . .

Court not a tyrant's favour, nor combine

To further his iniquitous design:

But, if your faith is pledg'd, though late and loth,

If covenants have pass'd between you both,

Never assassinate him! Keep your path!

But should he still misuse his lawless power

To trample on the people, and devour,

Depose or overturn him; anyhow!

Your oath permits it, and the gods allow . . . .

     Yet much I fear the faction and the strife,

Throughout our Grecian cities, raging rife,

And their wild councils. But do thou defend

This town of ours, our founder and our friend! . . .(6)

QUESTIONS

1.   Which of the documents deal explicitly with democracy as it has been defined?

2.   Which of the documents provides a positive depiction of democracy as you have come to understand it in this exercise? Read very carefully.

3.   Identify the document that discusses democracy, but does so in a most unfavorable way. Give specific examples to support your response. Characterize the tone of the author.

4.   Is there a document that is not about democracy at all? Which one is it? Are you able to determine what political theory it discusses? Based on what the author has said, define that system of government.

Endnotes

1. Joel Krieger, ed., <u>The Oxford Companion to Politics of the World</u> (New York: Oxford University Press, 1993), 220.

2. Walter T. K. Nugent, <u>Creative History: An Introduction to Historical Study</u>, The Lippincott History Series (Philadelphia: J. B. Lippincott Company, 1967), 71, 72.

3. <u>Ibid.</u>, 72-74.

4. Francis R. B. Godolphin, ed., <u>The Greek Historians</u>, Vol. II (New York: Random House, Inc., 1942), 633-37; 640-41.

5. <u>The Complete Writings of Thucydides, The Peloponnesian War</u>, trans. R. Crawley. The Modern Library (New York: Random House, 1934), 102-103.

6. George Howe and Gustave A. Harrer, eds., <u>Greek Literature in Translation</u>, J. H. Frere, trans. rev. ed., Preston H. Epps, ed. (New York: Harper and Brothers, 1948), 139-140.

Chapter IV
Change and Continuity in Similar Documents

On desperate seas long wont to roam,
Thy hyacinth hair, thy classic face,
Thy Naiad airs have brought me home,
To the glory that was Greece
And the grandeur that was Rome.(1)

"The grandeur that was Rome." Surely you have heard that line from the poem <u>To Helen</u> by Edgar Allan Poe on numerous occasions and in a variety of contexts. Why? What exactly was the grandeur that was Rome? Have you ever thought about it? What would compel a poet, ever so many centuries later, to write such a line? Certainly it must have been something extremely significant. Recall the introduction to this great civilization in your text. If you are unable to do so, return to those pages and reread them. What did you find? Many things obviously, but one is there repeatedly--the ability to govern. This ability, many would agree, was greatly augmented through not only the establishment of political institutions but law. Consider the importance of these two factors working together simultaneously. Clearly this combination is of great importance because one alone, as in the case of the Greeks, was a source of weakness. This proved to be especially true when large political entities like empires were established. In short, it might be fair to say that the Greeks were great political theoreticians while the Romans were great political practitioners. As the Oxford University classicist William Ward Fowler (1847-1921) said of them, "The Romans were, in fact, the most practical people in history; and this enabled them to supply what was wanting to the civilization of the Mediterranean basin in the work of the Greeks."(2)

An earlier exercise in the volume centered around a law code; the Code of Hammurabi. In light of the foregoing comments on Rome, it seems appropriate at this time to examine another set of laws--the Twelve Tables. Before discussing their origins it should be stated that you will be asked to examine yet another code of laws later on. The reasoning behind this should be rather self-evident to you. Obviously law codes are an extremely important historical source. They can tell you a great deal about a civilization and its people. Looking at them from a comparative perspective also enables you to reflect on how societies differ; how they are similar; and perhaps, provide some insight into how they evolve over time. Keep this in mind as you read the Twelve Tables with your dictionary at your side.

As for the Tables, best evidence tells us they were compiled somewhere between 451-449 B.C. by a special commission of ten patrician magistrates. Originally inscribed on twelve bronze plaques (thus their name), the Tables were destroyed in 390 B.C. by the invading Gauls. Drawn up in response to pressure exerted by the other class in the early Roman Republic (remember who they were?), the Twelve Tables are of fundamental importance in reconstructing the history of this ancient time period.(3)

DOCUMENT

Selections from the Twelve Tables

Table III: Execution; Law of Debt

When a debt has been acknowledged, or judgment about the matter has been pronounced in court, thirty days must be the legitimate time of grace. After that, the debtor may be arrested by laying on of hands. Bring him into court. If he does not satisfy the judgment, or no one in court offers himself as surety in his behalf, the creditor may take the defaulter with him. He may bind him either in stocks or fetters

. . . .

Unless they make a settlement, debtors shall be held in bond for sixty days. During that time they shall be brought before the praetor's court in the meeting place on three successive market days, and the amount for which they are judged liable shall be announced; on the third market day they shall suffer capital punishment or be delivered up for sale abroad, across the Tiber.

Table IV: Rights of Head of Family

Quickly kill . . . a dreadfully deformed child.

If a father thrice surrender a son for sale, the son shall be free from the father.

A child born ten months after the father's death will not be admitted into a legal inheritance.

Table V: Guardianship; Succession

Females shall remain in guardianship even when they have attained their majority.

If a man is raving mad, rightful authority over his person and chattels shall belong to his agnates or to his classmen.

A spendthrift is forbidden to exercise administration over his own goods . . . . A person who, being insane or a spendthrift, is prohibited from administering his own goods shall be under trusteeship of agnates.

Table VII: Rights Concerning Land

Branches of a tree may be lopped off all round to a height of more than 15 feet . . . . Should a tree on a neighbor's farm be bent crooked by a wind and lean over your farm, action may be taken for removal of that tree.

It is permitted to gather up fruit falling down on another man's farm.

Table VIII: Torts or Delicts

If any person has sung or composed against another person a song such as was causing slander or insult to another, he shall be clubbed to death.

If a person has maimed another's limb, let there be retaliation in kind unless he makes agreement for settlement with him.

Any person who destroys by burning any building or heap of corn deposited alongside a house shall be bound, scourged, and put to death by burning at the stake, provided that he has committed the said misdeed with malice aforethought; but if he shall have committed it by accident that is, by negligence, it is ordained that he repair the damage, or if he be too poor to be competent for such punishment, he shall receive a lighter chastisement.

Table IX: Public Law

The penalty shall be capital punishment for a judge or arbiter legally appointed who has been found guilty of receiving a bribe for giving a decision.

<u>Table XI: Supplementary Laws</u>

Intermarriage shall not take place between plebeians and patricians.(4)

QUESTIONS

After reading the introduction to this chapter and the document under investigation, you should be prepared to answer the questions that follow. Remember to write freely on the document pages as you use the procedures for analysis outlined in Chapter II.

1.   Do you remember the categories the historian uses to organize information? -- political, economic, social, religious, scientific, cultural, and intellectual. Which of these does the Twelve Tables address?

2.   Based on your study of the Roman Republic, are the Tables a good reflection of the society in question? How would you characterize that society using only the evidence in the document?

3.   Based on the evidence provided in the document, would you describe the Twelve Tables as a comprehensive code of laws, that is, one embracing both private and public life? Explain your thoughts in a short paragraph.

4.   Look back at the Code of Hammurabi. Compare and contrast the two documents. Clearly articulate the differences and similarities you find in them. Are these differences and similarities reflective of what you have learned about these two different civilizations? If you had a choice, under which code of laws would you prefer to live?

5.   After examining these two ancient law codes, do you have a better appreciation of your own legal system? Why?

Endnotes

1. The Oxford Dictionary of Quotations, 3rd ed., s.v. "Edgar Allan Poe 1809-1849."

2. W. W. Fowler, Rome (London: Williams and Norgate, 1912), 12, 55-59, 63.

3. M. Cary, A History of Rome Down to the Reign of Constantine (London: Macmillan & Co. LTD, 1965), 41-42.

4. Cicero, Laws, trans. C. W. Keys (Cambridge: Cambridge University Press, 1966) II, xii, 31.

Chapter V
Disagreeing With The Experts

At this point in your course of study, you should have examined two of the great religions of the world--Judaism and Christianity--along with a number of belief systems of other civilizations including Greek and Roman religion before the advent of Christianity and, prior to that, Zoroastrianism of the early Persians. Think back for a moment and try to recall anything about women in these religions. If you cannot, check the index of your text and reexamine the necessary pages with women in mind. Were women mentioned, and if so, in what context? How were they regarded? What role, if any, did women play in these religions--e.g., were they priestesses? Was there any sense of equality or inequality and on what premise was it based? These are important questions, if only in part because they continue to be issues debated within organized religion today.

Because it should be the most recently studied religion, the following exercise will focus on materials concerning Christianity and Paul of Tarsus (c.5 - c.67). Considered by many scholars to be the most important early Christian, Paul's attitudes regarding women and human sexuality continue to be debated. Dare to disagree with the experts as you examine the excerpts from the letters of St. Paul and two conflicting historical views. Have your dictionary by your side as you read the evidence and the questions that follow it. These questions should aid you in arriving at your own interpretation of Paul on women.

DOCUMENT 1

<u>St. Paul</u>

To the unmarried and to widows I would say this: it is an excellent thing if, like me, they remain as they are. Yet if they cannot contain, let them marry, for it is better to marry than to burn (with passion).(1)

Let those who have wives live as if they had none; let mourners live as though they were not mourning; let the joyful live as if they had no joy.

Man ought not cover his head, for he represents the likeness and supremacy of God; but woman represents the supremacy of man. Man was not made from woman, woman was made from man; and man was not created for woman, but woman for man. Therefore, in view of the angels, woman must wear a symbol of subjection on her head . . . . Is it proper for an unveiled woman to pray to God?(2)

Women must keep quiet at gatherings of the church. They are not allowed to speak, they must take a subordinate place, as the Law enjoins. If they want any information let them ask their husbands at home; it is disgraceful for a woman to speak in church.(3)

Wives, submit yourselves unto your own husbands, as unto the Lord.

For the husband is the head of the wife, even as Christ is the head of the church: and he is the saviour of the body.

Therefore as the church is subject unto Christ, so let the wives be to their own husbands in everything.

Husbands love your wives, even as Christ also loved the church, and gave himself for it;

That he might sanctify and cleanse it with the washing of water by the word,

That he might present it to himself a glorious church, not having spot, or wrinkle, or any such thing; but that it should be holy and without blemish.

34

So ought men to love their wives as their own bodies. He that loveth his wife loveth himself. For no man ever yet hated his own flesh; but nourisheth and cherisheth it, even as the Lord the church.

For we are members of his body, of his flesh, and of his bones.

For this cause shall a man leave his father and mother, and shall be joined unto his wife, and they two shall be one flesh.

This is a great mystery: but I speak concerning Christ and the church.

Nevertheless let every one of you in particular so love his wife even as himself; and the wife see that she reverence her husband.(4)

DOCUMENT 2

Charles Seltman, Women in Antiquity

Round about the middle of the 1st century of our era a new, idealistic, and utopian conception of the cosmos began to exert upon the civilised world a slow, levelling pressure . . . .

The observation has frequently been made that a [new] beginning . . . anti-feminism was due, in the first instance, to Paul of Tarsus . . . . Several factors require consideration: the background of Graeco-Roman civilisation, with its real respect for women; the legal status achieved by women and their ability to fill responsible posts in civil life; the continuing love of female beauty expressed alike by poets, painters, and sculptors; and, lastly, a freedom in matters of sex . . . .

For a variety of reasons, all this really appears to have been repugnant to Paul of Tarsus. Conceivably the circumstances leading to his conversion had something to do with his attitude . . . . It has been suggested that the time which he spent in Ephesus between A.D. 52 and A.D. 54 had something to do with crystallising his attitude toward women. In such circumstances, Paul, a genius in rebellion against society, was bound to run into trouble . . . . The letters to the Corinthians seem to reveal certain preoccupations that troubled Paul during his comparatively long residence in Ephesus. He had worries about money, idols, sex, and female liberty, and indeed he was most upset about sex and female liberty because he observed the absolute freedom, greater than anywhere else, enjoyed by the women of the city, and of all Ionia and Phrygia. But to Paul it all seemed great wickedness; and, endowed as he was with infinite courage, he dared to denounce it. His feeling came through in his letters from Ephesus to the churches of his foundation . . . .(5)

DOCUMENT 3

"Scholars Say Paul Wasn't Woman Hater"

That impassioned New Testament letter writer, Paul, often gets blamed by feminists these days for subordination of women. He's sometimes glibly denounced as a woman hater. But [some] scholars consider it a bum rap. They say that contrary to such popular images, Paul was a sensitive, affectionate man who recognized women's equal worth, whose views were ahead of his time, who worked closely with women and regularly extolled them.

"In his own time he was quite progressive about women," said the Rev. David Adams of Virginia Theological Seminary in Alexandria, Va., an Episcopal institution.

"He was very radical on their equality," Adams said. "To dismiss him as a misogynist . . . is just not so. He was not that at all."

Nevertheless, misinformed impressions of teachings considered by many scholars as mistakenly attributed to Paul sometimes get so warped that abusive husbands use them to justify beating their wives.

Claiming the Bible says wives are to be submissive, "they take the biblical text and distort it to support their right to batter," said U.S. Catholic bishops in condemning such domestic abuse of women. "A correct reading of Scripture leads people to a relationship based on mutuality and love."

The passage cited by the bishops as misused, Ephesians 5:21-33, apparently is not even Paul's. Scholars say that the books of Ephesians and Timothy, although purporting to be Paul's letters, have a distinctly different style and vocabulary than the huge corpus of authentic Pauline letters.

"Most scholars would say that the material is not from Paul himself," said Adams, a New Testament professor . . . .

But Adams said that while Paul expressed his basic radical stance on sexual equality, "there are other indications that at certain places he draws back . . . appropriating a kind of hierarchical view of society."

"It is fairly clear that he understood women were in a subordinate role, as did all of society," Adams said, adding this was "perfectly normal" in the historical context of Paul's culture.(6)

QUESTIONS

1. What is Paul's attitude about marriage and human sexual needs?

2. Can you determine the roles ascribed to men and women based on Paul's letters? On what foundation are these roles determined?

3. What did St. Paul describe as the proper relationship between husbands and wives? Are there conflicting points of view found in the selected excerpts? Is it possible to account for this variance of opinion?

4. What place did women have in the church, as outlined by Paul?

5. How do the historical interpretations of St. Paul differ?

6. Is it possible for you to determine how the historians in question arrived at their conclusions after reading Paul's actual letters yourself?

7. Now go ahead and do it--make your own interpretation of St. Paul on women. Do you think he was a product of his culture as the newspaper article states, or as Charles Seltman wrote in his book, Women in Antiquity, "a genius in rebellion against his society"?(7)

8. How is this exercise different from any other you have done so far? What kind of sources were used?

Endnotes

1. I Corinthians 7:8-9.

2. I Corinthians 11:7-15.

3. I Corinthians 14:34-35.

4. Ephesians 5:22-33.

5. Charles Seltman, <u>Women in Antiquity</u> (London: Thames and Hudson, 1956), 184-188.

6. "Scholars Say Paul Wasn't Woman Hater," <u>The Plain Dealer</u>, 6 July 1993.

7. Seltman, <u>Women in Antiquity</u>, 184-188.

Chapter VI
What Do You Believe?

Throughout the foregoing chapters of this book, a very conscious attempt has been made to illustrate the point that history is an ongoing process involving intellectual skills of the highest order. In other words, that it is not the mere memorization of information, or what you may have learned to think of as the facts. Consider that if this were the case, historians could not disagree on St. Paul's attitudes about women and human sexuality as you learned they do in the previous chapter.

Historians disagree for very important and complex reasons, all of which cannot be addressed in these small volumes. This disagreeing, or "the lesson of historical criticism," is in fact a form of subtle doubting. Why is it important for historians to do this and for you, as a student of history, to understand the ideas behind it? Think about this as you read the thoughts of the British historian, George Kitson Clark, quoted below:

> No man can escape from history or for long ignore it . . . . Whether he likes it or not the results of history, or what purport to be the results of history, or opinions coloured by beliefs about history, will invade his life and mind. He must be prepared for opinions about history or historical experience to have deeply affected the mind of anyone with whom he has dealings. This being so it is the act of a wise man to come to terms with what he cannot evade, and bring it, if he can, under control; that is he must try to get as near as he can to the reality in the history with which he is confronted, to test the cogency of the historical opinions which are likely to influence his mind, or the minds of anyone who is important to him, and perhaps winnow some of the nonsense out of them . . . . to do this he must become a <u>critical historian</u> . . . .(1)

That in fact, becoming a critical historian, is your task in this chapter as you examine the life and works of the great Byzantine scholar Procopius. Procopius was Byzantium's 6th century historian and he wrote fourteen volumes recording the personages, politics, building projects, and military campaigns of the Emperor Justinian. Consciously modeled after the renowned Greek historian Thucydides' work on the Peloponnesian Wars, these works present a laudatory account of the Emperor's achievements. Sometime in the middle of completion, Procopius paused to author another work with an entirely different point of view about his employer, Justinian. The Historia arcana, or Secret History, was a scurrilous attack on the Emperor, his wife Theodora, the military commander Belisarius and his wife, Antonina. This history assembled "every scrap of gossip, surmise, scandal, and slander about the empress and court." Purposefully kept from publication, the work came to light early in the 17th century.(2) What could account for such variance in interpretation? Using the skills of subtle doubting, decide which of these views is the most accurate. Be able to explain why as you examine the evidence provided.

DOCUMENT

Thus it was that Theodora, though born and brought up as I have related, rose to

royal dignity over all obstacles. For no thought of shame came to Justinian in

marrying her, though he might have taken his pick of the noblest born, most highly

educated, most modest, carefully nurtured, virtuous and beautiful virgins of all the

ladies in the whole Roman Empire: a maiden, as they say, with upstanding breasts.

Instead, he preferred to make his own what had been common to all men and,

careless of all her revealed history, took in wedlock a woman who was not only

guilty of every other contamination but boasted of her many abortions.

. . . .

And some of those who have been with Justinian at the palace late at night, men who were pure of spirit, have thought they saw a strange demoniac form taking his place. One man said that the Emperor suddenly rose from his throne and walked about, and indeed he was never wont to remain setting for long, and immediately Justinian's head vanished, while the rest of his body seemed to ebb and flow; whereat the beholder stood aghast and fearful, wondering if his eyes were deceiving him. But presently he perceived the vanished head filling out and joining the body again as strangely as it had left it.

. . . .

Later Mamilian also died. Anatolius's son-in-law, leaving one daughter who of course inherited his estate. While her mother was still living, this daughter too died, after marrying a man of distinction, by whom she had no children, male or female. Justinian immediately seized the whole estate, on the remarkable ground that it would be an unholy thing for the daughter of Anatolius, an old woman, to become rich on the property of both her father and her husband. But that the woman might not be reduced to beggary, he ordered her to be given one gold starter a day so long as she lived: writing in the decree by which he robbed her of these properties that he was granting her this starter for the sake of religion, "for it is my custom to do what is holy and pious."

. . . .

This, however, is worth telling among the innovations of Justinian and Theodora. Formerly, when the Senate approached the Emperor, it paid homage in the following manner . . . . It was not customary to pay homage to the Queen.

But those who were admitted to the presence of Justinian and Theodora, whether they were patricians or otherwise, fell on their faces on the floor, stretching their hands and feet out wide, kissed first one foot and then the other of the Augustus, and then retired. Nor did Theodora refuse this honor; and she even received the ambassadors of the Persians and other barbarians and gave them presents, as if she were in command of the Roman Empire: a thing that had never happened in all previous time.(3)

QUESTIONS

1.   Go to your own textbook and at least three others. Read what each has to say about Justinian, Theodora, and Procopius. Note the significant events in their lives; their backgrounds; and, their achievements.

2.   After reading the excerpts that precede these questions, find those things that cause you to either believe or doubt the accuracy of the <u>Secret History</u>. Don't forget to use your dictionary and to follow the steps for successful document reading.

3.   Procopius, Justinian, Theodora, all lived a very long time ago. Are these issues regarding how you interpret their lives important today? How have those in the employment of contemporary American Presidents dealt with these issues? Why would it be difficult to be a "court historian" and still engage in subtle doubting?

4.   An even more complex issue involved is the art of historical biography. In fact the matter is so thorny that another chapter will deal with it in depth. For now, think about the following quote and write a two hundred word essay agreeing or disagreeing with the thesis.

> . . . . The transgressive nature of biography is rarely acknowledged, but it is the only explanation for the biography's status as a popular genre. The reader's amazing tolerance . . . makes sense only when seen as a kind of collusion between him and the biographer in an exciting forbidden undertaking: tiptoeing down the corridor together, to stand in front of the bedroom door and try to peep through the keyhole.(4)

46

Endnotes

1. Geoge Kitson Clark, "The Critical Historian," <u>The Dimensions of History: Readings on the Nature of History and the Problems of Historical Interpretation</u>, ed. Thomas N. Guinsburg (Chicago: Rand McNally & Company), 17-18.

2. "Crowned Courtesan," <u>MD</u>, October 1966, 281.

3. Procopius, <u>Secret History of Procopius</u>, trans. Richard Atwater (Chicago: Pascal Covici Publisher, 1927), 111; 132; 266; and, 275.

4. Janet Malcolm, "The Silent Woman - I," <u>The New Yorker</u>, 23 & 30 August 1993, 86.

Chapter VII
Historical Generalization

In the two preceding chapters you have been grappling with issues centering on interpretation as a part of the historical process. Another extremely important component in this process is that of making generalizations. Can you define this term as it applies to history? Now read the following: "Theoretically, a historical generalization is a statement or term which has been inferred inductively from a number of particular cases, instances, or events."(1)

This definition of generalization should have taken you full circle intellectually-- right back to our beginning chapter where it was discovered that the definition of history meant a process of inquiry. To put this concisely, "the historical generalization suggests some regularity or pattern of events, ideas, and human actions which is of historical significance."(2)

Stop here and test your ability to recall and apply what you have learned from these exercises and the information in your text. What very famous ancient historian was attempting to use a historical generalization when he wrote "it will be enough for me . . . if these words of mine are judged useful by those who want to understand clearly the events which happened in the past and which (human nature being what it is) will at some time or other and in much the same ways, be repeated in the future. My work is not a piece of writing designed to meet the taste of an immediate public, but was done to last for ever."(3) Identify the generalization that has been made by rephrasing it in your own words.

Most historians agree that generalizations vary in gradations of inclusiveness. The simplest forms are one word labels--Jews, Christians, Muslims.(4) A more complex form of generalization serves to connect and interpret information. Obviously this level of use is extremely important for historical investigation. Not only does it put concepts and facts into meaningful relationship, it also helps to establish why and how certain events took place.(5)

Other forms of generalization operate at higher levels, but historians are not so prone to use them because they are quite unreliable. Our quote from Thucydides would be an example of a generalization of the highest degree of inclusiveness. Is he not seeking to find underlying principles of human behavior? Reread the quote.

Now examine the documents that follow. Each one is taken from three of the great religions in the world that you should have studied by this time in your course work. Follow the procedures you have used in the past as you work your way through the materials.

DOCUMENT 1

Psalm 8

O Lord, our Lord,

how majestic is thy name in all the earth!

Thou whose glory above the heavens is

    chanted

    by the mouth of babes and infants,

thou hast founded a bulwark because of thy

foes,

    to still the enemy and the avenger.

When I look at thy heavens, the work of thy

    fingers,

    the moon and the stars which thou hast

    established;

what is man that thou art mindful of him,

    and the son of man that thou dost care for

    him?

Yet thou hast made him little less than God,

    and dost crown him with glory and honor.

Thou hast given him dominion over the works

    of thy hands;

    thou hast put all things under his feet,

all sheep and oxen,

    and also the beasts of the field,

the birds of the air, and the fish of the sea,

whatever passes along the paths of the sea.

O Lord, our Lord

how majestic is thy name in all the earth!(6)

DOCUMENT 2

<u>The Gospel According to St. John</u>

In the beginning was the Word, and the Word was with God, and the Word was God. The same was in the beginning with God. All things were made by him; and without him was not any thing made that was made. In him was life; and the light of men. And the light shineth in darkness; and the darkness comprehended it not.

There was a man sent from God, whose name was John. The same came from a witness, to bear witness of the Light that all men through him might believe. He was not that Light, but was sent to bear witness of the Light, that all men through him might believe. That was the true Light, which lighteth every man that cometh into the world. He was in the world, and the world was made by him, and world knew not him. He came unto his own, and his own received him not. But as many as received him, to them gave he power to become the sons of God, even to them that believe on his name: which were born, not of blood, nor of the will of the flesh, nor of the will of man, but of God. And the Word was made flesh, and dwelt among us (and we beheld his glory, the glory as of the only begotten of the Father), full of grace and truth.(7)

DOCUMENT 3

The Koran

Say: HE IS ONE GOD:

God the Eternal.

He begetteth not, nor is begotten;

Nor is there one like unto Him.

Magnify the name of thy LORD, THE MOST HIGH,

Who created, and fashioned,

And decreed, and guided

Who bringeth forth the pasturage,

Then turneth it dry and brown.

We will make thee cry aloud, and thou shall not forget,

Except what God pleaseth; verily He knoweth the plain and hidden.

And will speed thee to ease.

Admonish, therefore--verily admonishing profiteth,--

Whoso feareth God will mind;

And there will turn away from it only the wretch

Who shall broil upon the mighty fire,

And then shall neither die therein, nor live.

Happy is he who purifieth himself,

And remembereth the name of his Lord, and prayeth.(8)

QUESTIONS

1.   How many generalizations are you able to make about the documents?

2.   Make different levels of generalizations from these documents. Is this more difficult to do? Think about the reasons and explain them in a paragraph or two.

3.   With the three documents in mind, read the quote provided below and identify the type of generalization it makes.

> Most men . . . do not think that men are all that matters.
> To think this is to run counter to a very deep feeling,
> namely, that man depends for life and fullness of being on
> forces outside himself that share in some sense his own
> nature and with which he must be in harmony. The
> harmony thus sought is sometimes a harmony in action . .
> . or it is a moral and spiritual harmony . . . or the harmony
> sought is more than a harmony, it is a complete and final
> identity . . . .(9)

4.   Based on your reading of the documents, would you maintain that the above quote is an accurate generalization? Explain why or why not.

Endnotes

1. Lester D. Stephens, <u>Probing the Past: A Guide to the Study and Teaching of History</u> (Boston: Allyn and Bacon, Inc., 1974), 66.

2. <u>Ibid</u>.

3. Thucydides, <u>History of the Peloponnesian Wars</u>, trans. Rex Warner (Harmondsworth, England: Penguin Books, 1972), 324.

4. Walter T. K. Nugent, <u>Creative History: An Introduction to Historical Study</u>, The Lippincott History Series (Philadelphia: J. B. Lippincott Company, 1967), 76.

5. Stephens, <u>Probing the Past</u>, 68.

6. Revised Standard Version of the Bible (Division of Christian Education of the National Council of the Churches of Christ in the USA, 1971).

7. George H. Knoles and Rixford K. Snyder, eds., <u>Readings in Western Civilization</u>, 3rd ed. (Chicago: J. B. Lippincott Company, 1960), 170.

8. Stanley Lane-Poole, <u>The Speech-and-Table-Talk of the Prophet Mohammed</u> (London: Macmillan, 1905), 15; 32; 83; 133-137.

9. John B. Noss, <u>Man's Religions</u>, 3rd ed. (New York: The Macmillan Company, 1963), 3.

Chapter VIII
Comparing and Contrasting Historical Documents

In his famous work <u>Germania</u> written in A.D. 98, the Roman senator, consul, and author Tacitus stated:

> It is a duty among them to adopt the feuds as well as the friendships of
> a father or a kinsman. These feuds are not implacable; even homicide
> is expiated by the payment of a certain number of cattle and of sheep,
> and the satisfaction is accepted by the entire family, greatly to the
> advantage of the state, since feuds are dangerous in proportion to a
> people's freedom.(1)

Specifically Tacitus was referring to the vendetta or blood feud, long a practice among the various Germanic tribes of Europe. Originating with Iron Age peoples between 800-500 B.C. in the southern reaches of Scandinavia and northern sections of central Europe, the Germans lived in a society where custom determined all behaviors. This, plus the fact that they could not write until converted to Christianity sometime late in the 6th century, leaves historians with little factual information except for authors such as Tacitus. His work, quoted above, is frequently referred to as a "conscious idealization of a primitive and unspoiled people calculated to chasten and reform the decadent Romans."(2)

However true this characterization, much of what this first century Roman historian wrote has proven invaluable to understanding the German way of life and the legal system that resulted from it. Having no concept of statehood as you understand it to exist in the world today, the Germans lived in a basic social unit called a tribe. The <u>folk</u>, members of the tribe, were all united by blood lineage that descended from a common ancestor. Kin protected kin and legal customs were passed down from generation to generation through oral tradition. Each tribe had its very own customs and all members were subject to its rule no matter where they traveled. Various tribes, especially when on friendly terms, respected one another's laws.

Ruled by tribal kings or chieftains, these selected male members represented the strongest from among the folk. The test of strength was determined in battle. Emerging in combat, he in turn led in combat, settled disputes among his members, offered sacrifices to the various gods, and negotiated with those outside his own unit.

Influenced by Christian missionaries and by the Romans with whom they mingled, German customs and life gradually changed. Much of this change is reflected in the various codes of law which the tribal leaders collected and recorded. These codes are not a coherent body of work, but rather an amended quilt--a works-in-progress, so to speak. Thus, they differ markedly from the previous law codes you have examined in this volume. Remember what they were? Right, the Code of Hammurabi and the Twelve Tables of the Roman Republic. You are reminded of these because in order to answer the questions in this chapter, it will be necessary to refer back to these earlier documents.

In the previous chapter dealing with laws codes, the focus was on change and continuity in similar source materials. These ideas will be taken further in this chapter by examining the important historical technique of comparing and contrasting information. As a student of history you are often asked to do this in an examination question. Your professor is trying to teach you how to use information in a comparative way. Examine the following questions. Every one deals with the same historical problem, but each is treated in a different way because of the verb:

QUESTIONS

1. <u>Discuss</u> the role of law in Western civilization. Use the Code of Hammurabi, the Roman Twelve Tables, and the Carolingian Capitulary Laws concerning Estates as the basis of your answer.

2. Trace the development of law in Western civilization using the Code of Hammurabi, the Roman Twelve Tables, and the Carolingian Capitulary Laws concerning Estates as your chief pieces of historical evidence.

3. Evaluate the role of law in Western civilization using the Code of Hammurabi, the Roman Twelve Tables, and the Carolingian Capitulary Laws concerning Estates as your examples.

4. Write an essay on the effectiveness of law in Western civilization. Make use of the following three law codes as your examples: The Code of Hammurabi; the Roman Twelve Tables; and, the Carolingian Capitulary Laws concerning Estates.

5. Compare and contrast the role of law in Western civilization by using the Code of Hammurabi, the Roman Twelve Tables, and the Carolingian Capitulary Laws concerning Estates.

Do you understand the importance of the point?

Interpret the documents that follow exactly as you have done in the past. Answer the questions that will be found after the documents.

DOCUMENT 1

Alfred the Great Blood Feuds

Also we enjoin, that a man who knows his adversary to be residing at home, shall

not have recourse to violence before demanding justice of him.

1. If he has power enough to surround his adversary and besiege him in his house, he shall keep him therein seven days, but he shall not fight against him if he (his adversary) will consent to remain inside (his residence). And if, after seven days, he will submit and hand over his weapons, he shall keep him unscathed for thirty days, and send formal notice of his position to his kinsmen and friends.

2. If, however, he flees to a church, the privileges of the church shall be respected, as we have declared above.

3. If, however, he has not power enough to besiege him in his house, he shall ride to the ealdorman and ask him for help. If he will not help him, he shall ride to the king before having recourse to violence.

4. And further, if anyone chances on his enemy, not having known him to be at home, and if he will give up his weapons, he shall be detained for thirty days, and his friends shall be informed (of his position). If he is not willing to give up his weapons, then violence may be used against him. If he is willing to surrender and hand over his weapons, and anyone after that uses violence against him (the pursued), he shall pay any sum which he incurs, whether

wergeld or compensation for wounds, as well as a fine, and his kinsmen shall forfeit his claim to protection as a result of his action.

5.   We further declare that a man may fight on behalf of his lord; if his lord is attacked, without becoming liable to vendetta. Under similar conditions a lord may fight on behalf of his man.

6.   In the same way a man may fight on behalf of one who is related to him by blood, if he is attacked unjustly, except it be against his lord. This we do not permit.

7.   A man may fight, without becoming liable to vendetta, if he finds another (man) with his wedded wife, within closed doors or under the same blanket; or (if he finds another man) with his legitimate daughter (or sister); or with his mother, if she has been given in lawful wedlock to his father.(3)

DOCUMENT 2

Salic Law

If any person strike another on the head so that the brain appears, and the three bones which lie above the brain shall project, he shall be sentenced to 1200 denars, which make 300 shillings . . .

If any one have killed a free woman after she has begun bearing children, he shall be sentenced to 2400 denars, which make 600 shillings . . . .

If any one shall have drawn a harrow through another's harvest after it has sprouted, or shall have gone through it with a wagon where there was no road, he shall be sentenced to 120 denars, which make 30 shillings . . . .

But if any one have slain a man who is in the service of the king, he shall be sentenced to 2400 denars, which make 600 shillings.(4)

QUESTIONS

1. What can you determine about Germanic society by examining their laws; of society in the Roman Republic under the Twelve Tables; in the society of Hammurabi?

2. How are the Germanic laws different from the early two codes of law? Account for these differences.

3. How are the German laws similar to the early two codes of law? Explain the similarities.

4. What concepts of abstract justice are included in these three law codes? Is it possible some are not based on such concepts? Can you explain why, based on the society(ies) in question?

5. Go further than the two examples of Germanic laws given and see what you can discover about the evolution of their various tribal laws. Do you find similar things in all of them as you compare and contrast them to the Code of Hammurabi and the Roman Twelve Tables? Consult "The Burgundian Code," trans. Katherine Fisher Drew (Philadelphia: University of Pennsylvania Press, 1949); David Herlihy, ed., Medieval Culture and Society (New York: Harper & Row, 1968).

62

Endnotes

1. Tacitus, <u>The Complete Works of Tacitus: The Annals o The History o The Life of Cnaeus Julius Agricola o Germany and Its Tribes o A Dialogue in Oratory</u>, ed. Moses Hadas, trans., Alfred John Church and William Jackson Brodribb, Modern Library Books (New York: Random House, Inc., 1942), 719.

2. Moses Brodribb, ed., <u>The Complete Works of Tacitus</u>, xii.

3. F. L. Attenborough, ed. and trans., <u>The Laws of the Earliest English Kings</u> (Cambridge: Cambridge University Press, 1922), 83-85.

4. E. F. Henderson, ed., <u>Select Historical Documents of the Middle Ages</u> (London: G. Gell & Sons, 1912), 176-189.

Chapter IX
Digging for Evidence

Make a list of sources you think some student a millenium from now would consult if he or she wished to discover the kinds of foods that were consumed in 20th century American society. Examine your list and see how many of those sources might have been available a millenium earlier. Not too many, right? Given you find this to be true, what source materials would you use to answer this important question about that period in time known generally as the Middle Ages? Below is a very brief list of possibilities:

1. Records from monasteries
2. Personal records and correspondence
3. Official records of knight's households
4. Guild records
5. Information about holiday and ceremonial feasts
6. Cooking manuals/cookbooks
7. Works of art
8. Poetry

Some of these possibilities should be of no surprise to you based on what you have already learned about this period in history. But what of the last three? Do you find it interesting to discover that cooking manuals or cookbooks existed? Did you assume they have always existed? One famous cooking manual, compiled by the master cooks of England's Richard II around 1390, was entitled The Forme of Cury. Here, for example, is a recipe for "salat": "Take parsel, sawge, garlec, chibollas . . . , oynons, leek, borage, myntes, porrectes . . . , fenel, and ton tressis . . . , rew, rosemarye, purslarye . . . ; lave, and woisshe hem clene; pike hem, pluk hem small with thyn . . . honde, and myng . . . hem ind raw oile. Lay on vynegar and salt, and serve it forth."(1)

A slightly older cookbook from France, a culture very often associated with excellent food, is that by Guillaume Tirel. Beginning as a mere scullion, he went on to work in the service of Philip VI of Valois and the Dauphin; was called to the kitchens of Charles V; and then, in 1375 wrote Le Viandier, the oldest French cookbook known to exist. Famous in its own day, it has remained so up to the present. In fact, Le Viandier is one of the first books to be put in print. Taillevent, as he liked to call himself, was much concerned with the secrets of making fine sauces, sops, and vegtables. Sops were an early form of pureed soups. They were made of wine flavored milk, saffron, and honey or other sweeteners. Dead at the age of sixty-nine, Taillevent was buried beneath a tombstone picturing him in the dress of a sergeant at arms. Appropriately, his shield was embellished with three cooking pots.(2)

Early or late in their appearance, cookbooks are a most obvious source of information about dietary preferences. Did you ever think the final two on the list of possibilities could yield this type of information? Go to your own textbook and several others to look for illustrations of medieval art. What did you find? If little, dig further. Visit your college or university library and seek out art histories of the period. Note the things you find and put them aside for now.

Poetry! Probably you never ever considered this as a source. Yet one of the greatest masterpieces of world literature, Chaucer's Canterbury Tales, says much about food. Examine the excerpts provided. Answer the questions that follow as you interpret Chaucer.

DOCUMENT

There also was a Nun, a Prioress,

Her way of smiling very simple and coy.

Her greatest oath was only 'By St Loy!'

And she was known as Madam Eglantyne.

And well she sang a service, with a fine

Intoning through her nose, as was most seemly,

And she spoke daintily in French, extremely,

After the school of Stratford-atte-Bowe;

French in the Paris style she did not know.

At meat her manners were well taught withal;

No morsel from her lips did she let fall,

Nor dipped her fingers in the sauce too deep;

But she could carry a morsel up and keep

The smallest drop from falling on her breast.

For courtliness she had a special zest,

And she would wipe her upper lip so clean

That not a trace of grease was to be seen

Upon the cup when she had drunk; to eat,

She reached a hand sedately for the meat.

She certainly was very entertaining,

Pleasant and friendly in her ways, and straining

To counterfeit a courtly kind of grace,

A stately bearing fitting to her place,

And to seem dignified in all her dealings.

As for her sympathies and tender feelings,

She was so charitably solicitous

She used to weep if she but saw a mouse

Caught in a trap, if it were dead or bleeding.

And she had little dogs she would be feeding

With roasted flesh, or milk, or fine white bread.

And bitterly she wept if one were dead

Or someone took a stick and made it smart;

She was all sentiment and tender heart. . . .

. . . .

A <u>Monk</u> there was, one of the finest sort

Who rode the country; hunting was his sport.

A manly man, to be an Abbot able;

Many a dainty horse he had in stable.

His bridle, when he rode, a man might hear

Jingling in a whistling wind as clear,

Aye, and as loud as does the chapel bell

Where my lord Monk was Prior of the cell.

The Rule of good St Benet or St Maur

As old and strict he tended to ignore;

He let go by the things of yesterday

And took the modern world's more spacious way.

He did not rate that text at a plucked hen

Which says that hunters are not holy men

And that a monk uncloistered is a mere

Fish out of water, flapping on the pier,

That is to say a monk out of his cloister.

That was a text he held not worth an oyster;

And I agreed and said his views were sound;

Was he to study till his head went round

Poring over books in cloisters? Must he toil

As Austin bade and till the very soil?

Was he to leave the world upon the shelf?

Let Austin have his labour to himself.

      This Monk was therefore a good man to horse;

Greyhounds he had, as swift as birds, to course.

Hunting a hare or riding at a fence

Was all his fun, he spared for no expense.

I saw his sleeves were garnished at the hand

With fine grey fur, the finest in the land,

And on his hood, to fasten it at his chin

He had a wrought-gold cunningly fashioned pin;

Into a lover's knot it seemed to pass.

His head was bald and shone like looking-glass;

So did his face, as if it had been greased.

He was a fat and personable priest;

His prominent eyeballs never seemed to settle.

They glittered like the flames beneath a kettle;

Supple his boots, his horse in fine condition.

He was a prelate fit for exhibition,

He was not pale like a tormented soul.

He liked a fat swan best, and roasted whole.

His palfrey was as brown as is a berry.

. . . .

There was a <u>Franklin</u> with him, it appeared;

White as a daisy-petal was his beard.

A sanguine man, high-coloured and benign,

He loved a morning sop of cake in wine.

He lived for pleasure and had always done,

For he was Epicurus' very son,

In whose opinion sensual delight

Was the one true felicity in sight.

As noted as St Julian was for bounty

He made his household free to all the County.

His bread, his ale were finest of the fine

And no one had a better stock of wine.

His house was never short of bake-meat pies,

Of fish and flesh, and these in such supplies

It positively snowed with meat and drink

And all the dainties that a man could think.

According to the seasons of the year

Changes of dish were ordered to appear.

He kept fat partridges in coops, beyond,

Many a bream and pike were in his pond.

Woe to the cook unless the sauce was hot

And sharp, or if he wasn't on the spot!

And in his hall a table stood arrayed

And ready all day long, with places laid. . . .(3)

QUESTIONS

1. What kinds of foods are mentioned in the <u>Tales</u>? Is there a considerable variety of food discussed in the poem? How many? List them.

2. Does it appear that food and drink are abundant? Does it seem that food and drink are important?

3. Find any descriptions of table manners. Describe them. Of what significance is this? How does it compare were someone to read this alongside Miss Manners or Emily Post?

4. Go back to the list of things you found when looking through your text and art books on the Middle Ages. How do these compare with what was in the <u>Canterbury Tales</u>? Write a brief essay on food and its importance in the Middle Ages.

5. If this topic is of particular interest to you, go further. Examine other works of poetry like <u>Carmina Burana</u>, and William Langland's <u>Piers the Ploughman</u>. Bon appetit!

72

Endnotes

1. William Harlan Hale and the editors of <u>Horizon Magazine</u>, <u>The Horizon Cookbook and Illustrated History of Eating and Drinking through the Ages</u> (Garden City, New York: American Heritage Publishing Co., Inc., 1968), 87.

2. <u>Ibid</u>., 85.

3. Geoffrey Chaucer, <u>The Canterbury Tales</u>, trans. Nevill Coghill (London: Penguin Books, 1951), 22-25; 28-29.

Chapter X
Visual and Written Sources: Piecing Together the Evidence

.

In many of the exercises you have undertaken so far, one or two sources have been the focus of concern. In every case they have involved some form of analysis using one form of evidence, usually a written document. Clearly the work of a practicing historian is much more multi-faceted. In fact, the number of sources consulted is vast and the types are often quite varied, depending greatly upon the topic under investigation.

Each source is a potential piece of evidence that the historian examines in light of the question(s) he or she is trying to answer. This intellectual trying out--a mind puzzle so to speak--involves asking questions of the source material. Does it fit in the puzzle? Does it support or refute the question(s); the hypothesis? Does it fit with other pieces of evidence already verified? How? Is the source reliable? Are there biases? If so what are they? These are but some of the important issues that must be addressed of every historical document.

Your task in this chapter is to examine evidence in at least two formats. The written evidence is provided for you on the next few pages of this workbook. The other options you may select from include the following: pictorial books featuring art of the Renaissance; a video; a trip to an art museum; the Internet. If you select a pictorial book consider one of these options--R.M. Letts, <u>The Cambridge Introduction to Art: The Renaissance</u>, B. Cole and A. Gealt, <u>Art of the Western World</u>, Chapters 6-8, or <u>The Horizon Book of the Renaissance</u>. If your choice is a video, view <u>Art of the Western World, Volume 2, The Early Renaissance</u> or <u>The High Renaissance</u>. Going to a museum is a wonderful choice, particularly if you live in a major city like Chicago, New York, Dallas, Cleveland, Washington, DC, Los Angeles, or San Francisco. By all means consider this option, especially if you have never been to a major art museum. Should the Internet be your option of choice, study a little book entitled <u>Internet Guide for History</u> by Daniel J. Kurland and John Soares. If you don't know anything about how to use the Internet, consult Mark E. Walker's, <u>How to Use the Internet</u>, Fourth Edition.

By now you certainly have determined that the historical period under investigation in this chapter in the Renaissance. This amazing time saw change of considerable magnitude in virtually every category used by historians when asking questions of their source materials. If you can't recall these, refresh you memory by returning to Chapter I of this volume. While you are doing that reflect on how amazed Renaissance thinkers, writers and artists would be at two of your options to study their work--a video and the Internet.

As you are probably aware, the literal definition of the work "Renaissance" is rebirth, and one of the consistent themes in this rebirth was humanism. Here is what you are to do. Arrive at a definition of this important term--humanism--by examining the two written documents that follow and two pictures that you select from the other options discussed in this introduction. Do you remember how to select as a historian? Return to Chapter III if necessary. Now answer the questions that are provided to help you.

DOCUMENT

Francesco Petrarch

[St. Augustine] . . . . But let us take for granted (what is quite impossible) that the duration of life will be long and assured: still, do you not find it is the height of madness to squander the best years and the best parts of your existence on pleasing only the eyes of the others and tickling other men's ears, and to keep the last and worst--the years that are almost good for nothing--that bring nothing but distaste for life and then its end--to keep these, I say, for God and yourself, as though the welfare of your soul were the last thing you cared for?

Even supposing the time were certain, is it not reversing the true order to put off the best to the last?

[Petrarch] I do not think my way of looking at it is so unreasonable as you imagine. My principle is that, as concerning the glory which we may hope for here below, it is right for us to seek while we are here below. One may expect to enjoy that other more radiant glory in heaven, when we shall have there arrived, and when one will have no more care or wish for the glory of earth. Therefore, as I think, it is in the true order that mortal men should first care for mortal things; and that to things transitory things eternal should succeed . . . .

[St. Augustine]   O man, little in yourself, and of little wisdom! Do you, then, dream that you shall enjoy every pleasure in heaven and earth, and everything will out turn fortunate and prosperous for you always and everywhere? But that delusion has betrayed thousands of men thousands of times, and has sunk into hell a countless host of souls. Thinking to have one foot on earth and one in heaven, they could neither stand here below nor mount on high. Therefore they fell miserably, and the moving breeze swept them suddenly away, some in the flower of their age, and some when they were in midst of their years and all their business.

[Petrarch] . . . . I will be true to myself, so far as in me lies. I will put myself together and collect my scattered wits, and make to great endeavour to possess my soul in patience. But even while we speak, a crowd of important affairs, though only of the world, is waiting my attention.

[St. Augustine]   For the common herd of men these may be what to them seem more important; but in reality there is nothing of more importance, and nothing ought to be esteemed of so much worth. For, of other trains of thought, you may reckon them to be not essential for the soul, but the end of life will prove that these we have been engaged in are of eternal necessity . . . .(1)

Pico Della Mirandola

Hear then, oh Fathers precisely what this condition of man is; and in the name of your humanity, grant me your benign audition as I pursue this theme.

God the Father, the Mightiest Architect, had already raised, according to the precepts of His hidden wisdom, this world we see, the cosmic dwelling of divinity, a temple most august. He had already adorned the supercelestial region with Intelligences, infused the heavenly globes with the life of immortal souls and set the fermenting dung-heap of the inferior world teeming with every form of animal life. But when this work was done, the Divine Artificer still longed for some creature which might comprehend the meaning of so vast an achievement, which might be moved with love at its beauty and smitten with awe at its grandeur. When, conse-quently, all else had been completed . . . , in the very last place, He bethought

Himself of bringing forth man. Truth was, however, that there remained no archetype according to which He might fashion a new offspring, nor in His treasure-houses the wherewithal to endow a new son with a fitting inheritance, nor any place, among the seats of the universe, where this new creature might dispose himself to contemplate the world. All space was already filled; all things had been distributed in the highest, the middle and the lowest orders. Still, it was not in the nature of the power of the Father to fail . . . .

At last, the Supreme Maker decreed that this creature, to whom He could give nothing wholly his own, should have a share in the particular endowment of every other creature. Taking man, therefore, this creature of indeterminate image, He set him in the middle of the world and thus spoke to him:

"We have given you, Oh Adam, no visage proper to yourself, nor any endowment properly your own, in order that whatever place, whatever form, whatever gifts you may, with premeditation, select, these same you may have and possess through your own judgment and decision. The nature of all other creatures is defined and restricted within laws which We have laid down; you, by contrast, impeded by no such restrictions, may, by your own free will, to whose custody We have assigned you, trace for yourself the lineaments of your own nature. I have placed you at the very center of the world, so that from that vantage point you may with greater ease glance round about you on all that the world contains. We have made you a creature neither of heaven nor of earth, neither mortal nor immortal, in order that you may, as the free and proud shaper of your own being, fashion yourself in the form you may prefer. It will be in your power to descend to the lower, brutish forms of life; you will be able, through your own decision, to rise again to the superior orders whose life is divine.(2)

QUESTIONS

1. Identify the category of history around which this exercise revolves. Did you have to look them up in Chapter I? Explain why you picked this category.

2. What salient trends do you find articulated in the written documents? The first was written by Francesco Petrarch (1304-1374) and the second by Giovanni Pico Della Mirandola (1463-1494). List these trends. Briefly define and discuss each.

3. Turn your attention to the two pictures you have selected from the pictorial sources, video, museum visit, or the Internet. Identify the artist for each picture. Were you familiar with both of them? If not, you might investigate a little into their lives. Do you find the same trends in the pictures you selected as you identified in the previously examined written documents? Write a paragraph about each identified trend and explain how they are found in both the pictures and the written documents.

4. Define "humanism" using the evidence you have gathered from your four pieces of evidence. Look up the word in your text and compare both definitions. How well did you do?

5. Visit a good library. Look up the topic "the Renaissance" and select two of the volumes listed. Examine the bibliography at the end. Approximate the number of sources the author consulted. Look again to see if he or she used more than written source materials. What were they?

Endnotes

1.   Francesco Petrarca, <u>Petrarca's Secret, or the Soul's Conflict with Passion,</u> trans. William H. Draper (London: Chatto & Windus, 1911), 175-192.

2.   G. Pico Della Mirandola, <u>Oration on the Dignity of Man</u>, trans. A. R. Caponigri (Chicago: Gateway, 1956), 1-5.

Chapter XI
An Invaluable Historical Helpmate--Maps

Did you ever wonder why the Western Hemisphere is not called North Columbus, Central Columbus, South Columbus rather than North America, Central America, South America? Consider that this might be due to information you have at your fingertips and thus take for granted. Specifically, think of something as ordinary as a map. "To regain a sense of what a map once meant, to see it as a document whose borders reflect the cognitive borders of its makers, all we have to do is examine contemporary maps of the universe which . . . are still very much works-in-progress." Put this into an even better perspective by realizing that as recently as January of 1996, "astronomers learned to their dismay that they were forty billion galaxies short of the actual total, which is around fifty billion--a re-evaluation unparalleled since the explorations of the early 16th century that forever altered man's conception of the known world."(1)

Although it would be incorrect to say that Christopher Columbus had no maps, not to mention considerable experience and the best of the then prevailing knowledge of the world, important aspects of this information were incorrect. During the Age of Discovery, map-making tended to follow the successes of the seafarers and their respective nations. The conception Columbus had of the world was represented in a map produced in 1489 by one Henricus Marcellus. True, Marcellus had included important new information acquired after the Portuguese sailor, Bartholomew Diaz, had successfully rounded the Cape of Good Hope, at the southern tip of Africa, in the year 1488. However, Marcellus made no attempt to estimate the size of the ocean that separated the east coast of Africa and the west coast of Europe. Columbus was also incumbered by a compendium of errors coming from a complilation of maps and text by the Alexandrian scholar Claudius Ptolemaeus

(127-160 A.D.). Ptolemy's <u>Geography</u>, as it is commonly known, made the earth "out to be too small, taking 45 nautical miles as one degree at the equator instead of the true 59.5 miles."(2) The <u>Geography</u> also extended the land mass of Asia much further eastward than is correct.

Believing that he had arrived in Asia until his death in 1506 at the age of fifty-five, Columbus' four voyages therefore brought no changes in cartographical depictions of the world. Instead, that would come in 1507 when a German map maker, Martin Waldseemuller would designate the new continent "America" after Americo Vespucci. Under the flag of Portugal, this Italian sailor had explored the eastern coast of South America at the dawn of the new century.(3) Given that you have this information to work with, carefully examine excerpts from the two letters that follow. Proceed to answer the questions that follow.

DOCUMENT 1

Knowing that it will afford you pleasure to learn that I have brought my undertaking to a successful termination, I have decided upon writing you this letter . . . . Thirty-three days after my departure from Cadiz I reached the Indian Sea where I discovered many islands, thickly peopled, of which I took possession without resistance in the name of our most illustrious Monarch . . . . This said island of Juana is exceedingly fertile, as indeed are all the others; it is surrounded with many bays, spacious, very secure, and surpassing any that I have ever seen; numerous large and healthful rivers intersect it, and it also contains many lofty mountains. All these islands are very beautiful, and distinguished by a diversity of scenery; they are filled with a great variety of trees of immense height, and which I believe to retain their foliage in all seasons; for when I saw them they were as verdant and luxuriant as they are in Spain in the month of May . . . . The nightingale and various birds were singing in countless numbers, and that in November . . . . In that land also which I have before said we named Espanola, there are mountains of very great size and beauty, vast plains, groves, and very fruitful fields admirably adapted for tillage, pasture, and habitation. The convenience and excellence of the harbours in this island, and the abundance of the rivers, so indispensable to the health of man, surpass anything that would be believed by one who had not seen it. The trees, herbage, and fruits of Espanola are very different from those of Juana, and moreover it abounds in various kinds of spices, gold, and other metals . . . . [The natives] exhibit great love towards all others in preference to themselves: they also give objects of great value for trifles, and content themselves with very little or nothing in return. I however forbad that these trifles and articles of no value (such as pieces of dishes, plates, glass, keys, and leather straps) should be given to them, although if they could obtain them, they imagined themselves to be possessed of the most beautiful trinkets in the world. . . . Thus they bartered, like idiots, cotton and gold for fragments of bows, glasses, bottles, and jars; which I forbad as being unjust, and myself gave them many beautiful and acceptable articles which I had brought with me, taking [nothing] from them in return. I did this in order that I might more easily conciliate them that they might be led to become Christians, and be inclined to entertain a regard for the King and Queen, our Princes and all Spaniards, and that I might induce them to take an interest in seeking out, and collecting, and delivering to us such things as they possessed in abundance, but which we greatly needed . . . (4)

DOCUMENT 2

On a former occasion I wrote to you at some length concerning my return from those new regions whch we found and explored with the fleet, at the cost, and by the command of the Most Serene King of Portugal. And these we may rightly call a new world. Because our ancestors had no knowledge of them, and it will be a matter wholly new to all those who hear about them. For this transcends the view held by our ancients, inasmuch as most of them hold that there is no continent to the south beyond the equator, but only the sea which they named the Atlantic; and if some of them did aver that a continent there was, they denied with abundant argument that it was a habitable land. But that this their opinion is false and utterly opposed to the truth, this my last voyage has made manifest for in those southern parts I have found a continent more densely peopled and abounding in animals than our Europe or Asia or Africa, and, in addition, a climate milder and more delightful than in any other region know to us. . .(5)

QUESTIONS

1. What do each of the men think they have discovered? Examine some early maps in your textbook or others to better understand their importance. Better yet, consult a work by A. L. Humphreys, Antique Maps and Charts (New York: Dorset Press, 1989).

2. Compare and contrast the observations made by the two seafarers by constructing a chart. Include categories like exaggeration; accuracies; inaccuracies; levels of excitement.

3. Were these men keen observers? Were there any motivating reasons behind the accounts they made--e.g. political, economic?

4. Further explore the importance and development of map making. Read Arthur Krystal's insightful article entitled, "All the World's A Map," Art & Antiques, August 1996, 59-65.

Endnotes

1.   Arthur Krystal, "All the World's A Map," <u>Art & Antiques</u>, August 1996, 60.

2.   Ray Ginger, <u>People on the Move: A United States History</u> (Boston: Allyn and Bacon, Inc., 1975), 4-5.

3.   Krystal, "All the World's A Map," 63.

4.   Philip F. Alexander, ed., <u>The Discovery of America, 1492-1584</u> (London: Cambridge University Press, 1917), 1-9.

5.   Amerigo Vespucci, <u>Mundus Novus</u>, trans. George Tyler Northrup, "Vespucci Reprints, Texts, and Studies," Vol. V (Princeton, New Jersey: Princeton University Press, 1916), 1.

Chapter XII
Discovering Something New about Someone Well-Known

Despite the fact that his parents were peasant folk, they were better off than most. This enabled him to attend a university where he completed his courses in the liberal arts. He began to study the law as his father had a very practical bent. Abruptly he changed his mind and entered the Augustinian Eremites order. Two years later he was a priest.

Plagued by terrible doubts regarding his spiritual worthiness, the young man devoted himself to excessive forms of asceticism. Relief was not forthcoming. Around 1515, when in the course of lecturing to his university students, he found the answer. There it was in St. Paul's Epistle to the Romans--"The just shall live by faith." Have you figured out by now who this is? Correct, Martin Luther!

This is just some of the information you might have learned in your past or very recent study of Luther and the first part of the Reformation. Surely your list would also include: indulgences; the Ninety-Five Theses; The Address to the Christian Nobility of the German Nation on the Improvement of the Christian Estate; the Diet of Worms; and, the Lutheran Church. Probably you could list considerably more. Do you think you know all there is to know about Luther? Are you familiar with Luther's views on matters pertaining to marriage? Are you aware that he married Katherine von Bora, a former nun, and that they had a family? Perhaps this is shocking to you, but realize that celibacy was not always a vow required of Church leaders. Refer back to St. Paul in Chapter VI and recall that Peter had a wife. This is known because the other disciples referred to his mother-in-law. After the Lutheran Reformation, marriage came to be accepted and expected for all Protestants.

87

Read on by examining Luther's views on this still important religious issue. See what new information you can acquire about an already known figure in history. An important thing to keep in mind is the worth of reading the ideas of the actual individual who initiated them. Interesting, isn't it?; this was Luther's view on the Bible and part of his reason for translating the New Testament into German.(1)

DOCUMENT

Grace and peace in Christ, our Lord and Savior. You are not the only ones . .

. . I myself am greatly plagued by them; I put up a stiff resistance, calling and

crying out that these things should be left to the temporal authorities, and as Christ

says, "Leave the dead to bury their own dead" [Matt. 8:22]. God grant that they may

do this, rightly or wrongly, for we are supposed to be servants of Christ, that is, we

are to deal with the gospel and conscience, which gives us more than enough to do

against the devil, the world, and the flesh.

No one can deny that marriage is an external, worldly matter, like clothing

and food, house and property, subject to temporal authority. Nor do I find any

examples in the New Testament where Christ or the apostles concerned themselves

with such matters, except where they touched upon consciences . . . .

Therefore I simply do not wish to become involved in such matters at all and

beg everyone not to bother me with them. If you do not have sovereigns, then you have officials. If they do not render just decisions, what concern is it of mine. They are responsible, they have undertaken the office. I am horrified too by the example of the pope, who was the first to get mixed up in this business and has seized worldly matters as his own to the point where he has become nothing but a worldly lord over emperors and kings . . . .

Now the whole world knows (praise God) what effort and zeal I have already expended and how hard I am still toiling to see that the two authorities or realms, the temporal and the spiritual, are kept distince and separate from each other and that each is specifically instructed and restricted to its own task. The papacy has so jumbled these two together and confused them with each other that neither one has kept to its power or force or rights and no one can disentangle them again. This is what I dread and with God's help I want to avoid it and stay within the charge of my own office . . . .

But since you persist so strongly in asking instruction of me . . . I will not withhold my opinion from you. Yet I give it with this condition (which I hereby wish to have stated clearly to you and to everyone), that I want to do this not as a judge, official, or regent, but by way of advice, such as I would in good conscience give as a special service to my good friends . . . . Let whoever is supposed to rule or wants to rule be the ruler; I want to instruct and console consciences, and advise them as much as I can. Whoever wishes to or can comply, let him do so; whoever will not or can not, let him refrain . . . .

The First Article

Secret engagements should not be the basis of any marriage whatsoever.

The Second Article

A secret engagement should yield to a public one.

The Third Article

Of two public engagements, the second should yield to the first and be punished.

The Fourth Article

If anyone touches another woman after a public engagement, so to marry her in order thereby to break the first engagement, this action is to be regarded as adultery.

The Fifth Article

Forced engagements should not be valid.

First, the divine law, that because marriage is a public estate which is to be entered into and recognized before the church, it is fitting that it should also be established and begun publicly with witnesses who can testify to it, for God says, "Every word should be confirmed by the evidence of two or three witnesses" [Matt. 18:16] . . . .

Second, we also have here the temporal imperial law which clearly forbids such secret betrothals. Now in our external conduct we are bound to obey the temporal law. We should not cause the imperial laws to yield and subjugate themselves to papal laws because these same papal laws often run counter to public ordinances, reason, and good sense.

Third, this is also confirmed by the ancient canons and by the best points of the canon law, all of which forbids such secret engagements . . . .

Fourth, add to this the example of the old law and all the fathers among whom it was both law and custom that the parents gave their children in marriage by parental authority, as is clearly stated in Exodus 21, and as the examples of Isaac, Jacob, Joseph, Samson, etc., show.

Fifth, it was also in the natural law among the heathen, and also with the Greeks, who were the wisest people on earth. We read these words in the works of the Greek poet Euripides, "It is my father's business to arrange for my marriage. It is not fitting that I have anything to do with it." St. Ambrose finds this passage very pleasing . . . .

Forced engagements should not be valid.

The whole world is unanimous in this article, for God has created man and woman so that they are to come together with pleasure, willingly and gladly with all their hearts. And bridal love or the will to marry is a natural thing, implanted and inspired by God. This is the reason bridal love is so highly praised in the Scriptures and is often cited as an example of Christ and his church . . . . The Holy Spirit did not cause such an example to be written down in vain; he wished by this to confirm the natural law, which he created in such a way that marriage partners are to be joined together without force or compulsion, but willingly and with pleasure.

. . . .

Necessity demands that we also say something about divorce . . . . We have heard above that death is the only reason for dissolving a marriage. And because God has commanded in the law of Moses that adulterers should be stoned, it is certain that adultery also dissolves a marriage . . . .

Accordingly, I cannot and may not deny that where one spouse commits adultery and it can be publicly proven, the other partner is free and can obtain a divorce and marry another man. However, it is a great deal better to reconcile them and keep them together if possible. But if the innocent partner does not wish to do this, then let him in God's name exercise his right. And above all, this separation is not to take place on one's own authority, but it is to be declared through the advice and judgment of the pastor or authorities . . . .

But in order that such divorces may be as few in number as possible, one should not permit the one partner to remarry immediately, but he should wait at least a year or six months. Otherwise it would have the evil appearance that he was happy and pleased that his spouse had committed adultery and was joyfully seizing the opportunity to get rid of this one and quickly take another and so practice his wantonness under the cloak of the law . . . .(2)

QUESTIONS

1. What advice does Luther give to other ministers regarding marriage? On what does he base his advice?

2. What are his views on marriage? How did they differ with the Roman Catholic Church?

3. Is Luther anti-authority? Explain your response by giving specific examples in a paragraph each. On what source does Luther base his opinions?

4. Are you able to detect Luther's views on marital intimacy? Discuss them. Return to Chapter VI and examine the writing of St. Paul. How are St. Paul's and Luther's views on this subject similar or dissimilar?

5. What are Luther's views on divorce? Examine these as well as those discussed about with the recent Roman Catholic Bishops "Pastoral Familial Directorate" and Pope John Paul II's encyclical "Veritatis Splendor."

Endnotes

1. Wallace K. Ferguson and Geoffrey Brunn, <u>A Survey of European Civiliza-tion</u>, 3rd ed. (New York: Houghton Mifflin Company, 1962), 377-382.

2. Robert C. Shultz, ed., <u>The Christian in Society</u>, Vol. 3. (Philadelphia: Fortress Press, 1967).

Chapter XIII
Looking Twice at the Same Person

The long reign of Louis the XIV (1643-1715) brought to fruition the work of Cardinal Richelieu in his endeavors to strengthen royal power. It was in France, under the rule of the "Sun King," that there emerged a highly developed centralized state. Disorder and insecurity were gradually replaced by religious uniformity, state policy coordinated by mercantilism, and glorification of power. These were the hallmarks of 17th century European civilization and France had one of the most impressive practitioners in Louis.

With dictionary in hand, read through Louis XIV's conception of royal responsibility to his son. Absolutism and skills in reading autobiography are your concern in this important document. Answer each of the questions that follow the document.

DOCUMENT

Two things without doubt were absolutely necessary: very hard work on my part, and a wise choice of persons capable of seconding it ....

I laid a rule on myself to work regularly twice every day, and for two or three hours each time with different persons, without counting the hours which I passed privately and alone, nor the time which I was able to give on particular occasions to any special affairs that might arise. There was no moment when I did not permit people to talk to me about them provided they were urgent . . . .

I cannot tell you what fruit I gathered immediately I had taken this resolution. I felt myself, as it were, uplifted in thought and courage; I found myself quite another man, and with joy reproached myself for having been too long unaware of it. This first timidity, which a little self-judgment always produces and which at the beginning gave me pain, especially on occasions when I had to speak in public, disappeared in no time. The only thing I felt then was that I was King, and born to be one. I experience next a delicious feeling, hard to express, and which you will not know yourself except by tasting it as I have done.

For you must not imagine, my son, that the affairs of State are like some obscure and thorny path of learning, which may possibly have already wearied you, wherein the mind strives to raise itself with effort above its purview, repugnant to us as much as its difficulty. The function of Kings consists principally in allowing good sense to act, which always acts naturally and without effort. What we apply ourselves to is sometimes less difficult than what we do only for our amusement. Its usefulness always follows. A King, however skillful and enlightened be his minis- ters, cannot put his own hand to the work without its effects being seen. Success, which is agreeable in everything, even in the smallest matters, gratifies us in these as

well as in the greatest, and there is no satisfaction to equal that of noting every day

some progress in glorious and lofty enterprises, and in the happiness of the people

which has been planned and thought out by oneself. All that is most necessary to

this work is at the same time agreeable; for, in a word, my son, it is to have one's

eyes open to the whole earth; to learn each hour the news concerning every province

and every nation, the secrets of every court, the mood and the weaknesses of every

Prince and of every foreign minister; to be well-informed on an infinite number of

matters about which we are supposed to know nothing; to elicit from our subjects

what they hide from us with the greatest care; to discover interests of those who

come to us with quite contrary professions. I do not know of any other pleasure we

would not renounce for that . . . .

QUESTIONS

1. What particulars does Louis XIV believe are important for his son to rule effectively? How are they representative of the 17th century hallmarks previously articulated?

2. Read through the document again and make a list of what you find admirable about Louis XIV.

3. Read the document for a third time and compile a list of these aspects of Louis you dislike.

4. Compare your two lists and write a two paragraph essay (a biographical vignette) on Louis. Is your vignette well-balanced? Is good biography a balanced presentation? Is real balance possible or does a biographer already have strong opinions about his or her subject? Think about your answer the next time you read a biography.

Endnotes

1.   <u>A King's Lessons in Statecraft: Louis XIV; Letters to His Heirs</u>, Vol. II trans. Herbert Wilson (London: Ernest Benn Limited, 1924), 48-50.

DOCUMENTS

Chapter II

The Code of Hammurabi
From Cohn-Haft, Louis, ed., Source Readings in Ancient History, Vol. I: The Ancient Near East and Greece. Copyright (c) 1965 by Macmillan Publishing Company.

Chapter III

From The Greek Historians by Francis R. B. Godolphin. Copyright (c) 1942 by Random House, Inc. Reprinted by permission of Random House, Inc. From The Complete Writings of Thucydides by Thucydides Copyright (c) 1951 by Random House, Inc. Reprinted with permission of Random House, Inc. From Greek Literature in Translation by George Howe and Gustave A. Harrer, eds. rev. ed. Copyright (c) 1948. Reprinted by permission of Harper/Collins Publishers, Inc.

Chapter IV

The Twelve Tables
From Laws by Cicero, trans. by C. W. Keys. Copyright (c) 1966 by Cambridge University Press. Reprinted by permission of Cambridge University Press.

Chapter V

Reprinted from the Holy Bible. New International Version. From Women in Antiquity by Charles Seltman. Copyright (c) 1956 by Thames and Hudson LTD. Reprinted by permission of Thames and Hudson LTD. "Scholars Say Paul Wasn't A Woman Hater," The Plain Dealer, 6 July 1993. Reprinted from The Plain Dealer.

Chapter VI

From <u>Secret History of Procopius</u> by Procopius, trans. by Richard Atwater, Copyright (c) 1927. Pascal Covici Publisher.

Chapter VII

From the Holy Bible. Revised Standard Version of the Bible. "The Gospel According to St. John," page 170. From <u>Readings in Western Civilization</u> by George H. Noles and Rixford K. Snyder. Copyright (c) 1960 by Harper & Row, Inc. Copyright renewed. Reprinted by permission of Harper/Collins Publishers, Inc. Reproduced with the permission of Macmillan Publishing Company, Inc. From <u>The Speech-and-Table-Talk of the Prophet Mohammed</u> by Stanley Lane-Poole. Copyright (c) 1905 by Macmillan Publishing Company.

Chapter VIII

<u>Alfred the Great Blood Feuds</u>
From <u>The Laws of the Earliest English Kings</u>. F. L. Attenborough, ed. and trans. Copyright (c) 1922 by Cambridge University Press. Reprinted by permission of Cambridge University Press.
<u>Salic Law</u>
From <u>Select Historical Documents of the Middle Ages</u>. E. F. Henderson, ed. Copyright (c) 1912 by G. Gell & Sons. Reprinted by permission of Harper/Collins Publishers, Inc.

Chapter IX

From <u>The Canterbury Tales</u>, by Geoffrey Chaucer, translated by Nevill Coghill. Copyright (c) 1951 by Penguin Classics. Reprinted with permission of Penguin Books, Ltd.

Chapter X

From <u>Petrarca's Secret, or the Soul's Conflict with Passion</u> by Francesco Petrarca, trans. by William H. Draper. Chatto & Windus LTD. Random House UK LTD. From <u>Oration on the Dignity of Man</u> by G. Pico Della Mirandola, trans. by A. R. Caponigri. Copyright(c) 1956. Gateway.

Chapter XI

From <u>The Discovery of America, 1492-1584</u>, ed. by Philip F. Alexander. Copyright (c) 1917 by Cambridge University Press. Reprinted by permission of Cambridge University Press. From Amerigo Vespucci, <u>Mundus Novus</u>, trans. George Tyler Northrup, "Vespucci Reprints, Texts, and Studies," Vol. V. Copyright (c) 1916 by Princeton University Press. Reprinted by permission of Princeton University Press.

Chapter XII

Reprinted from <u>The Christian in Society</u> by Robert C. Schultz. Copyright (c) 1967 Fortress Press. Used by permission by Augsburg Fortress.

Chapter XIII

From <u>A King's Lessons in Statecraft: Louis XIV: Letters to His Heirs, Vol. II</u>, trans. by Herbert Wilson. Copyright (c) 1924 Ernest Benn Limited. Reprinted by permission of A & C Black Publishers Limited.